P9-DOB-376

A Primary Source Guide to

JAPAN

Tobi Stanton Stewart

The Rosen Publishing Group's

PowerKids Press™
PRIMARY SOURCE

LIBRARY
FRANKLIN PIERCE COLLEGE
RINDGE NH 03461

New York

Published in 2003 by The Rosen Publishing Group, Inc.
29 East 21st Street, New York, NY 10010

Copyright © 2003 by The Rosen Publishing Group, Inc.

All rights reserved. No part of this book may be reproduced in any form without permission in writing from the publisher, except by a reviewer.

Book Design: Haley Wilson

Photo Credits: Cover, p. 1 © The Image Bank; p. 4 (map) © Map Resources; p. 4 (inset) © Michael S. Yamashita/Corbis; p. 6 (Mount Fuji) © Roger Ressmeyer/Corbis; p. 6 (inset) © Sakamoto Photo Research Laboratory/Corbis; p. 8 (shrine inset) © Dallas & John Heaton/Corbis; pp. 8, 10 (inset) © Bettmann/Corbis; p. 10 © Corbis; p. 12 © Pablo Corral IV/Corbis; p. 13 © Reuters NewMedia Inc./Corbis; p. 14 © Charles Gupton/Stone; p. 16 © Jack Fields/Corbis; p. 18 © Burstein Collection/Corbis; p. 20 © Bob Rowan, Progressive Image/Corbis; p. 22 © EyeWire.

Library of Congress Cataloging-in-Publication Data

Stewart, Tobi Stanton.
  A primary source guide to Japan / Tobi stanton stewart.
       p. cm.
Summary: Text and photographs reveal the culture, history, artifacts,
and traditions of the eastern Asian nation, Japan, which is made up of
several thousand islands in the North Pacific Ocean.
  ISBN 0-8239-6594-5 (library binding)
  ISBN 0-8239-8078-2 (pbk.)
  6-pack ISBN: 0-8239-8085-5
  1. Japan—Juvenile literature. 2. Japan—Pictorial works—Juvenile
literature. [1. Japan.] I. Title.
  DS806 .S478 2003
  952—dc21
                                        2002004926

Manufactured in the United States of America

Contents

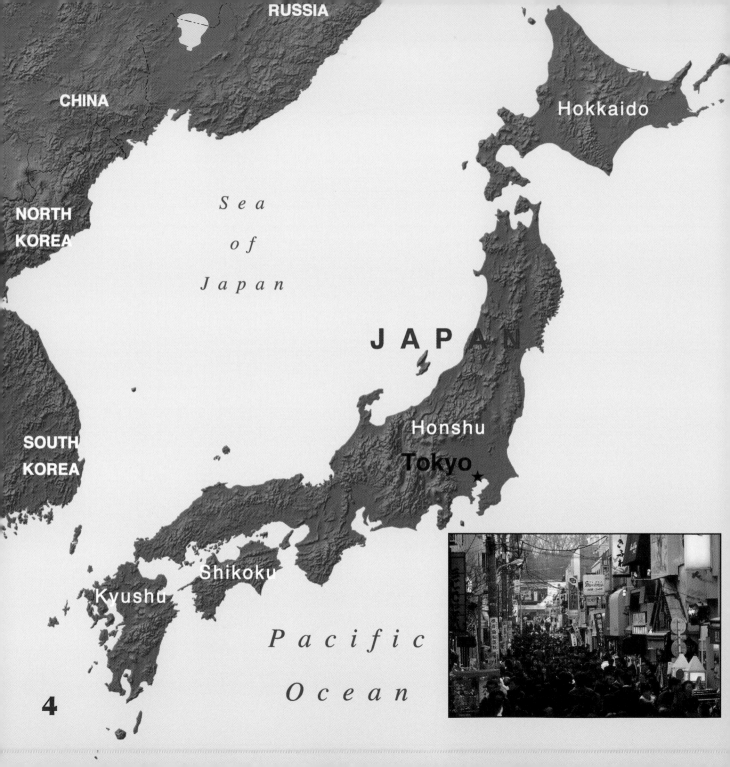

RUSSIA

CHINA

Hokkaido

NORTH
KOREA

Sea

of

Japan

JAPAN

SOUTH
KOREA

Honshu

Tokyo

Shikoku

Kyushu

Pacific

Ocean

4

A Look at Japan

Japan is a country in Asia. It is made up of several thousand islands off the Asian mainland in the Pacific Ocean. Japan's four largest islands are Hokkaido, Honshu, Shikoku, and Kyushu. Most of Japan's 126 million people live on these four main islands. About four-fifths of the people in Japan live in crowded cities.

Tokyo is the capital of Japan. It is also Japan's largest city. About 12 million people live in Tokyo. About 18 million more people live in the area around Tokyo.

Japan is a small country with a large population. Overcrowding is often a problem. About one-fourth of all the people in Japan live in the Tokyo area, shown in the small picture on the left.

A Land of Mountains

Japan's land is mostly rocky and mountainous. The most famous mountain in Japan is Mount Fuji, which is southwest of Tokyo. At more than 12,000 feet (3,658 meters) tall, it is Japan's highest mountain. Japan also has low plains near its coasts. Most people live on this flatter land.

Central and southern Japan have hot summers, mild winters, and steady rainfall throughout the year. The weather is much cooler in northern Japan and high in the mountains. Japan is sometimes hit by typhoons. A typhoon is a storm with strong winds and a lot of rain.

◀ Throughout history, many Japanese people have thought of Mount Fuji as a holy mountain. It has been a favorite subject of Japanese art for centuries. This painting was done in the early 1800s by a Japanese artist. Japanese art often has poems and other writing on it.

The Emperor's Changing Role

Japan's first emperor was crowned around 660 B.C. The emperor had unlimited power and was treated like a god. Today, Japan still has an emperor, but his role has changed. He is the **symbol** of Japan and its people, but he does not control the government.

In Japan, men and women over the age of twenty can vote for members of the Diet. "Diet" is the name for Japan's **parliament**, a group of leaders chosen by the people to make laws for the country. The leader of the government is the **prime minister**. The prime minister is chosen by the Diet.

◀ This photograph of Emperor Hirohito was taken in 1928. He wears the robe he wore when he was officially crowned emperor of Japan that year, a title he held until his death in 1989. The building in the small photo is a copy of the palace that Japanese emperors lived in hundreds of years ago.

9

Signed at TOKYO BAY, JAPAN at 0904. I
on the ___SECOND___ day of ___SEPTEMBER___, 1945.

重光 葵

By Command and in behalf of the Emperor of Japan
and the Japanese Government.

梅津 美治郎

By Command and in behalf of the Japanese
Imperial General Headquarters.

Accepted at TOKYO BAY, JAPAN at 0908 I
on the ___SECOND___ day of ___SEPTEMBER___, 1945,
for the United States, Republic of China, United Kingdom and the
Union of Soviet Socialist Republics, and in the interests of the other
United Nations at war with Japan.

Douglas Mac Arthur
Supreme Commander for the Allied Powers.

C.W. Nimitz
United States Representative

徐永昌
Republic of China Representative

Bruce Fraser.
United Kingdom Representative

Tengene -untenam R.Dyrhant
Union of Soviet Socialist Republics
Representative

CABlamey
Commonwealth of Australia Representative

Moore Cosgrove.
Dominion of Canada Representative

Leclerc
Provisional Government of the French
Republic Representative

M.Kerfivre
Kingdom of the Netherlands Representative

Leonard M Isitt
Dominion of New Zealand Representative

10

A Turning Point for Japan

In the 1930s, Japan's military leaders took over the government, hoping to conquer new lands. In 1941, Japan attacked a United States military base at Pearl Harbor in Hawaii. This brought the United States into World War II. In 1945, the United States dropped two **atomic bombs** on Japan, destroying two cities and killing tens of thousands of people. Japan **surrendered**.

The Japanese had to work hard to recover from the war. By the 1970s, Japan was once again a powerful nation with a successful economy.

◀ Atomic bombs were dropped on Hiroshima and Nagasaki in August 1945. The small photo was taken in Nagasaki after the bombs were dropped. The document is part of a treaty of surrender Japan signed on September 2, 1945, aboard a United States ship called the U.S.S. *Missouri* in Tokyo Bay.

A Strong Economy

Japan's economy is one of the strongest in the world. The people of Japan make many products, such as cars, computers, steel, TVs, and stereos. Japan trades its products with many countries, including the United States. More than one-quarter of Japan's **exports** go to the United States.

Most of Japan's people live very well. Many people have high-paying jobs. In Tokyo, the streets are lined with tall, expensive apartment buildings and fancy shops.

◀ This photo shows the front and back of Japanese money, which is called "yen."

◀ Japan is one of the largest car producers in the world. This photo shows a Japanese car being made.

13

Life in Japan

Japanese is the official language of Japan, but many people also speak English. Education is very important in Japan. Students are encouraged by their families to do their best in school.

Family life is also very important in Japan. Grandparents often live with the family. People celebrate aging because they believe older people are very wise. Many Japanese families eat their meals together. Meals often include rice, fish, and tea. Some people sit on pillows on the floor to eat and talk. At night, many people sleep on padded mats. In the morning, the mats are rolled up and put away.

◀ Like the family shown here, most Japanese people take off their shoes before they enter a home. This is considered good manners.

Shinto and Buddhism

Japan's two main religions are Shinto and Buddhism. It is common for people to follow both religions. Shinto means "the way of the gods" and honors gods that are found everywhere in nature. Buddhism is based on the teachings of a man named Buddha. Buddha said that life is a series of many deaths and rebirths. Everyone's place in life depends on their actions in earlier lives.

Buddhists have **festivals** throughout the year. They celebrate Buddha's birthday by decorating their temples with flowers and pouring tea over statues of the baby Buddha.

◄ Some of the finest Japanese sculptures are found in Buddhist temples. The most famous bronze statue in Japan, seen here, is called "the Great Buddha." It was made during the 1200s.

Art in Japan

Japan is close to China and has been affected by Chinese civilization. Early Japanese artists borrowed ideas from Chinese art. They painted **scrolls** which told stories using a series of pictures. They also created simple pictures using black ink on a white background. Later, artists cut designs into wooden blocks, rubbed the blocks with ink, and pressed paper against the blocks to make prints.

Many Japanese buildings are also works of art. The Japanese believe that buildings should be a part of the natural beauty around them. They use a simple building style to create harmony with nature.

◄ Japanese ink paintings like the one shown here were popular from the 1300s through the 1500s. About 100 years later, wood-block prints became popular. Some Japanese art is even decorated with very thin sheets of gold!

Japan Today

Japan is rich in history, but its people look toward the future. The people of Japan work together to help the country grow both socially and economically. Japan's economy has grown quickly since World War II, largely from exporting valuable manufactured goods to other countries. As a result, Japan's cities have become larger and more modern.

The Japanese people have made many advances in science and **technology**. Some scientists in Japan try to find cures for sicknesses. Others invent new products for us to use in our everyday lives.

◀ Japan's young people are important to the country's future. Japanese students study math, science, social studies, and the Japanese language, as well as art and music. Many students also learn English and attend school six days a week for eleven months a year!

Japan at a Glance

Population: About 126,000,000
Capital City: Tokyo (population about 12,000,000)
Largest City: Tokyo
Official Name: Nippon
National Anthem: "Kimigayo"
("The Reign of Our Emperor")
Land Area: 145,870 square miles
(377,801 square kilometers)
Government: Parliamentary democracy
Unit of Money: Yen
Flag: Japan's flag is white
with a red sun. The
Japanese call their country
Nippon, which means
"source of the sun."

Glossary

atomic bomb (uh-TAH-mik BAHM) A very strong bomb that can destroy large areas and poison the air, land, and water for many years to come.

export (EK-sport) Something that is sent out of one country for sale and use in another country.

festival (FESS-tuh-vuhl) A day or special time during which an important person or event is honored.

parliament (PAHR-luh-muhnt) A group of leaders chosen by the people to make laws for a country.

prime minister (PRYM MIH-nuh-stir) The highest official in some governments.

scroll (SKROHL) A roll of paper with writing or images on it.

surrender (suh-REHN-duhr) To stop fighting and give up.

symbol (SIM-buhl) Something that stands for something else.

technology (tek-NAH-luh-jee) The use of scientific knowledge to solve problems and to find new and better ways to do things.

Index

Primary Source List

Page 6. *Red Mount Fuji*. Hanging scroll painted by Noro Kaiseki (1747–1828), with text in upper left corner. Calligraphy was an art form, and Japanese paintings and prints commonly included poems and other text.

Page 8 (large image). Photograph of Emperor Hirohito in coronation robe. Taken November 10, 1928, when Hirohito was officially crowned emperor.

Page 8 (inset). Heian Shrine, Kyoto, built 1895. Smaller-scale replica of first Imperial Palace, built in 794 A.D.

Page 10 (large image). Japanese Instrument of Surrender. Signed in Tokyo Bay aboard the U.S.S. *Missouri*, September 2, 1945. Original in National Archives, Washington, D.C.

Page 10 (inset). Mother and son eating in a shack surrounded by rubble, Nagasaki. Photograph taken September 14, 1945.

Page 13. 2,000-yen banknote. Shown on the front of the note is the Shurei Gate of Shuri Castle in Okinawa, Japan. Shown on the back of the note is an illustration from the ancient Japanese novel *Tale of Genji*.

Page 16. Bronze *Daibutsu*, or colossal statue of Buddha, about thirty-seven feet high, by Tanji Hisamoto, 1252. In Kotokuin Temple, Kamakura.

Page 18. *Autumn Landscape*. Hanging scroll, ink painting on paper by Sesshu Toyo (1420–1506).

Web Sites

Due to the changing nature of Internet links, The Rosen Publishing Group, Inc. has developed an on-line list of Web sites related to the subjects of this book. This site is updated regularly. Please use this link to access the list:
http://www.powerkidslinks.com/pswc/psja/

Franklin Pierce College Library

00146048

DATE DUE

MAY 1 8 2005

NOV 0 4 2005

FEB 1 4 2006

ILL# 739568866   3/12/11 VCN

PRINTED IN U.S.A.

GAYLORD